Y0-BZE-387

FOCUS ON CLIMATE ZONES

POLAR CLIMATES

Cath Senker

capstone

© 2017 Heinemann Raintree
an imprint of Capstone Global Library, LLC
Chicago, Illinois

To contact Capstone Global Library, please call 800-747-4992, or visit our web site www.capstonepub.com

All rights reserved. No part of this publication may be reproduced or transmitted in any form or by any means, electronic or mechanical, including photocopying, recording, taping, or any information storage and retrieval system, without permission in writing from the publisher.

Edited by Linda Staniford
Designed by Philippa Jenkins
Original illustrations © Capstone Global Library Limited 2017
Illustrated by Oxford Designers and Illustrators, and Gordon Hurden p 5
Picture research by Svetlana Zhurkin
Production by Victoria Fitzgerald
Originated by Capstone Global Library Ltd

20 19 18 17 16
10 9 8 7 6 5 4 3 2 1

Library of Congress Cataloging-in-Publication Data
Library of Congress Cataloging-in-Publication Data is available on the Library of Congress website.
ISBN: 978-1-4846-3784-5 (library hardcover)
ISBN: 978-1-4846-3788-3 (paperback)
ISBN: 978-1-4846-3800-2 (eBook PDF)

This book has been officially leveled using the F&P Text Level Gradient™ Levelling System.

Acknowledgments
We would like to thank the following for permission to reproduce photographs: Alamy: Kevin Schafer, 42; Capstone: Gordon Hurden, 5 (top), Oxford Designers and Illustrators, 16, 17 (left); Chris Linder, 40; Eric Larsen, 24; Getty Images: Gabe Rogel, 44; iStockphoto: troutnut, 31; Minden Pictures: Flip Nicklin, 20, Todd Mintz, 17 (right); NASA Earth Observatory, 11, 38; NASA: JPL, 9; National Geographic Creative: Cory Richards, 8; Newscom: Danita Delimont Photography/Cindy Miller Hopkins, 23, EPA/Angelika Warmuth, 30, ITAR-TASS/Denis Kozhevnikov, 29, ZUMA Press/David Woodfall, 26, ZUMA Press/Gary Braasch, 15; Ryan Waters, 25; Shutterstock: Anibal Trejo, 7, Arina Borevich, 12, Armin Rose, 45, bikeriderlondon, 39, Capricornis Photographic, 19, Christian Wilkinson, 21, ciapix, cover, Dale Lorna Jacobsen, 43, David Gaylor, 28, Dmytro Pylypenko, 27, 32, 41, gans33, 14, Kris Grabiec, 13, 34, Maxim Tupikov, 5 (bottom), Ondrej Prosicky, 18, Sam Chadwick, 35, Supertrooper, back cover and throughout, wildestanimal, 36, Yongyut Kumsri, 33; Wikimedia: NASA Earth Observatory, 37

We would like to thank Dr Sandra Mather, Professor Emerita, Department of Geology and Astronomy, West Chester University, West Chester, Pennsylvania, USA, for her invaluable help in the preparation of this book.

Every effort has been made to contact copyright holders of material reproduced in this book. Any omissions will be rectified in subsequent printings if notice is given to the publisher.

All the Internet addresses (URLs) given in this book were valid at the time of going to press. However, due to the dynamic nature of the Internet, some addresses may have changed, or sites may have changed or ceased to exist since publication. While the author and publisher regret any inconvenience this may cause readers, no responsibility for any such changes can be accepted by either the author or the publisher.

TABLE OF CONTENTS

Some words are shown in bold, **like this**. You can find out what they mean by looking in the glossary.

WHERE ARE THE POLAR CLIMATE ZONES?

At the northern and southern extremes of Earth lie the polar climate zones. Surrounding the North Pole is the Arctic, the northern polar region. Around the South Pole is the southern polar region — the continent of Antarctica.

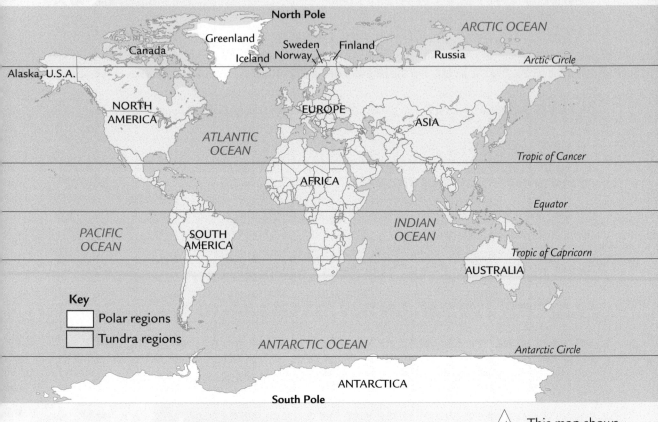

This map shows the polar and tundra regions of the world.

ICE CAP AND TUNDRA

Around the North and South Poles there is a polar climate, the coldest of all the climates on the planet. At the northern edges of North America, Europe, and Asia, the **tundra** climate is a little less chilly than at the poles. In the tundra, the upper few centimeters of the land defrost in summer, but the ground below remains frozen all year round. This frozen layer is called permafrost.

Amazing fact

The Arctic includes parts of eight countries: Canada, the United States, Iceland, Greenland, Norway, Sweden, Finland, and Russia. Nobody lives permanently in Antarctica.

Why is it so cold?

The Sun's rays do not strike Earth directly at the polar regions as they do at the **Equator.** The warmth of the Sun barely reaches the poles.

SURVIVAL IN THE SNOW

Some plants have adapted to survive with little sunshine or rain. Animals roam the land or swim in the oceans with fur or **blubber** for protection against the elements. Some people brave the freezing temperatures to make their homes here.

Now, climate change is raising temperatures at the icy poles more rapidly than anywhere else on the planet. In this journey to the poles, we will learn about life in the polar climate zones and discover how changes here could affect everyone.

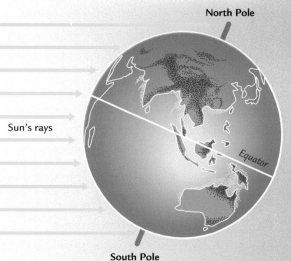

North Pole

Sun's rays

Equator

South Pole

The polar regions get no direct sunlight because the Sun's rays hit the land at an angle. The rays are spread over a wide area. This means the polar regions receive less heat than other parts of the world.

DID YOU KNOW?

Most people probably only see ice in the winter. Large parts of Antarctica and Greenland are covered in **ice sheets** all year round, while much of the Arctic Ocean has a thin layer of sea ice floating on it.

WHAT IS THE POLAR CLIMATE LIKE?

The polar climate is one of the most hostile on Earth. It's bitterly cold and the ground is covered in thick snow and ice. There are just two seasons — summer and winter. The weather forecast is almost always the same: cold, cold, and more cold.

Large, permanent expanses of ice reflect the Sun's weak rays. These ice sheets cool the water around them and the air above them, lowering the temperature more. In the middle of Antarctica, winter temperatures have dropped to an unbelievably low −135.8° Fahrenheit (−93.2° Celsius).

WINTER AND SUMMER

The Arctic summer lasts from June to August. In Antarctica, summer appears briefly from January to February. But even in summer, the temperature rarely rises above 32°F (0°C) at the polar **ice caps.**

The polar tundra is a bit milder: in the winter, temperatures "only" drop to −70°F (−57°C). In summer, average temperatures go up to 50°F (10°C) in July. It's like early spring in Illinois. That's as warm as it ever gets!

These charts show the temperature and rainfall in Yakutsk, Russia, the coldest city in the world.

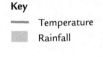

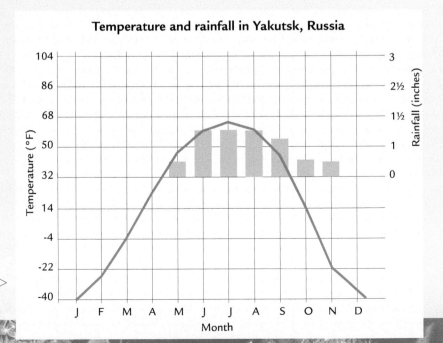

Amazing fact

Polar scientists have been known to dash outside naked when it's -100°F (-73°C)! Humans can survive such temperatures for about three minutes.

The city of Tromso in Norway is in the "land of the midnight sun." On summer nights, people can go walking and cycling or even swim.

DAY AND NIGHT

Day and night at the poles are as extreme as the temperatures. A place's **latitude** determines the amount of daylight it has. Being farthest from the Equator, the poles have barely any daylight in midwinter. At midsummer, the poles are bathed in sunlight almost 24 hours a day. That's why the Arctic is known as the "land of the midnight sun." Sounds great for a summer party? Sadly, it's way too cold.

WINDS

Not only is it freezing cold at the poles, but there are also fierce winds blowing.

Winds flow around our planet in particular patterns. They're called **prevailing winds**. Polar easterlies are cold, dry winds blowing from the east. They blow around the North and South Poles. Antarctica is one of the windiest places on the planet. Howling winds called katabatics batter the region from high mountains down to the valleys below.

HIGH AND DRY

Altitude also affects the temperature. The higher you go, the colder it gets. The center of Antarctica is at an average height of nearly 2 miles (3,000 meters). The skies are clear blue and snowfall is rare, just several inches a year. It's way too cold for rain. This means that Antarctica is a desert. In fact, it's the largest desert in the world.

Queen Maud Land in Antarctica experiences wild winds. The highest winds ever recorded in Antarctica were in July 1972. They reached 199 mph (327 kph).

WATER ON THE MOVE

Ocean **currents** also help to control climate. Just as air moves around in winds, water flows around the oceans in currents. Scientists call it the global ocean conveyor belt. Warm water flows from the Equator toward the polar regions, and cold water moves from the poles back to the Equator. The oceans help to spread heat around the globe. Without them, the extremes of temperature in our world would be even greater: super hot at the Equator and even colder at the poles.

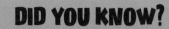

DID YOU KNOW?

Floating pack ice covers much of the Arctic Ocean. It is made from many individual islands of ice and is hundreds of miles wide. The islands grind together as they move.

Here you can see how the global ocean conveyor belt works, moving water around the world to bring cold water to warm areas and warm water to cold areas.

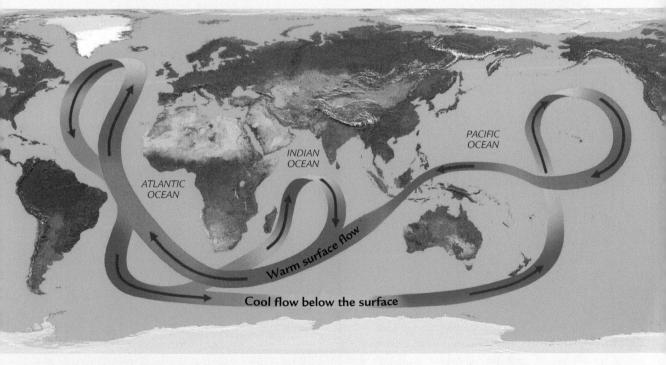

PACIFIC OCEAN

INDIAN OCEAN

ATLANTIC OCEAN

Warm surface flow

Cool flow below the surface

EYEWITNESS — A SUB-ANTARCTIC VOLCANO ERUPTS

In early 2016, a team of scientists was sailing near Heard Island, about 2,500 miles (4,000 kilometers) southwest of Australia. The little island has an active volcano called Big Ben. Although it erupts quite often — at least three times between 2000 and 2016 — it's so remote that few people have seen it in action. Usually, researchers only spot the eruptions later when viewing satellite images.

The scientists were on an expedition led by the University of Tasmania. They were learning about the effect of iron from underwater volcanoes on phytoplankton in the Southern Ocean. Phytoplankton are tiny ocean plants that provide food for many sea creatures, such as whales and jellyfish. Just as the ships approached, the volcano began to erupt.

This map shows the location of remote Heard Island. Big Ben makes up most of the island.

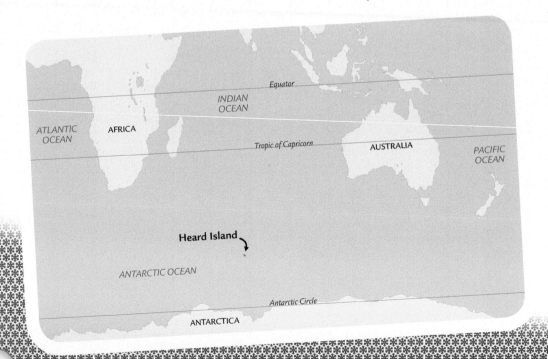

Equator

INDIAN OCEAN

ATLANTIC OCEAN

AFRICA

Tropic of Capricorn

AUSTRALIA

PACIFIC OCEAN

Heard Island

ANTARCTIC OCEAN

Antarctic Circle

ANTARCTICA

Amazing fact

Under Antarctica, active volcanoes are contributing to global warming. West Antarctica is particularly affected; scientists even discovered a new volcano there in 2013. In the areas with volcanoes, the ice is melting faster than elsewhere on the continent.

FIRE AND ICE

Professor Mike Coffin, the chief scientist on the voyage, described the extraordinary scene: "We saw vapor being emitted from the top of the volcano and we saw lava flows coming down the flank of Big Ben. This was a very exciting observation." It was quite incredible to watch because the island is covered in ice. Fiery lava flowed dramatically down the icy mountain. Coffin and his colleagues captured the awesome event on video for the world to see.

Bristol Island in Antarctica is also made up of active volcanoes, one of which erupted spectacularly in May 2016.

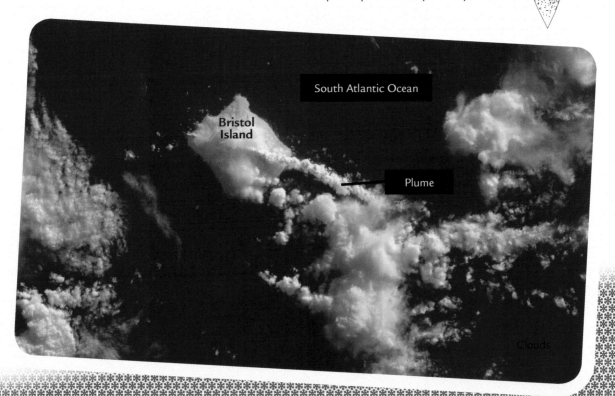

South Atlantic Ocean

Bristol Island

Plume

Clouds

WHICH PLANTS LIVE IN THE POLAR REGIONS?

Plants have to be specially adapted to survive the polar climate. At the polar ice caps, no plants can grow. There are no trees anywhere in the polar regions. There isn't enough soil to support large plants, it's too cold, and the growing season is too short. The ground is mostly frozen all year. Only the top layer of the soil thaws and refreezes each year.

ARCTIC TUNDRA

Away from the North Pole, in the Arctic tundra, **mosses** and **lichen** add color to the landscape. These simple plants can grow on the ground and even on stones.

Mosses (on the left) and lichen (on the right) are some of the most common tundra plants. These plants are growing in Karelia, a region in northern Finland and Russia.

Plants with shallow root systems are able to survive in the thin layer of soil available to them. Grasses, dwarf shrubs, and small flowering plants appear. Tundra flowering plants are small — often just a few inches tall. They cluster near the ground to reduce damage from the cold weather and harsh winds. The pasqueflower and the bearberry have silky hairs to protect them from drying winds.

Saxifrage is one of the very first flowers to bloom in the Arctic spring.

Winter and summer flowers

Many polar plants have adapted to the long winter. Some, such as the tiny, star-shaped purple flowers of saxifrage, can grow under a layer of snow. Tundra plants can photosynthesize (make their food from carbon dioxide in the air, water, and sunlight) in extremely low temperatures.

Tundra plants grow fast in the short summer. They use the long sunlight hours to produce flowers and seeds before winter arrives again.

DID YOU KNOW?
Some tundra plants have fuzzy coverings on their stems, leaves, and buds to protect them from the cold.

Adapted for cold

Take a look at polar flowers: their shapes and colors are adapted to the cold climate. The Arctic poppy has cup-like flowers that direct the Sun's rays to the middle of the flower. Others, such as the Arctic willow, are a dark color to absorb as much of the weak sunlight as possible.

Some tundra plants have adapted to polar climates by developing short stems and flowers that grow close to the ground, out of the wind. The Alpine saxifrage flower nestles within a rosette, or circle, of leaves for protection.

This polar poppy is growing in Novaya Zemlya, northern Russia. The flowers grow among stones, which absorb the Sun's warmth, and they always turn to face the Sun to get as much heat as possible.

Energy savers

Many tundra plants are **perennials.** They grow and flower in summer, die back in winter, then grow again the next year. This means they don't need to use energy producing seeds. Others multiply via root growth — this means that a whole new plant can grow from a root.

Amazing fact

So much of Antarctica is covered in snow and ice that it's only possible for plants to grow on 1 percent of the land.

ANTARCTIC PLANTS

In the Antarctic, plants have to cope with a lack of water as well as subzero temperatures. Antarctica has just two native "true" plants (with leaves, stems, roots): Antarctic hair grass and Antarctic pearlwort. They grow near the west coast of the Antarctic Peninsula, where temperatures are milder.

The region is also home to about 300 types of moss, more than 300 types of **algae** on land, and about 150 species of lichen. Lichen and algae grow inside crevices in the rocks, where there is a little water. It's easier to survive in these sheltered places than to endure the strong winds on the surface.

Hair grass is usually found in penguin colonies and manages to survive the high winds and large amounts of penguin poo!

WHICH ANIMALS LIVE IN THE ARCTIC AND ANTARCTIC?

The temperatures are subzero and the landscape is wild. Bitter winds blow and the hours of winter darkness are long. Yet the lands and oceans of the polar regions are rich in wildlife.

AMAZING ADAPTATIONS

Animals have developed amazing adaptations to cope in the treacherous polar climates. They have thick fur and layers of fat to keep them warm or are **camouflaged** against the snow to hide from predators or to sneak up on prey. Some live in caves or burrow in holes in the ground for shelter. Grazing animals eat the sparse plants and in turn are hunted by carnivores (animals that eat meat). Some animals migrate (move) to warmer climates for the coldest months. Others **hibernate** to save energy.

ARCTIC FOOD CHAINS

Lichen, moss, and shrubs grow on the land, providing food for caribou (a kind of reindeer), rabbits, and other grazing animals. Grazing animals are eaten by Arctic foxes. Polar bears, wolves, and eagles prey on Arctic foxes as well as grazing animals.

This is a typical food chain on Arctic land. Foxes also eat lemmings (small rodents) and young birds.

polar bear   wolf   snowy owl

Arctic fox

caribou   musk ox   rabbit

lichen   moss   grass

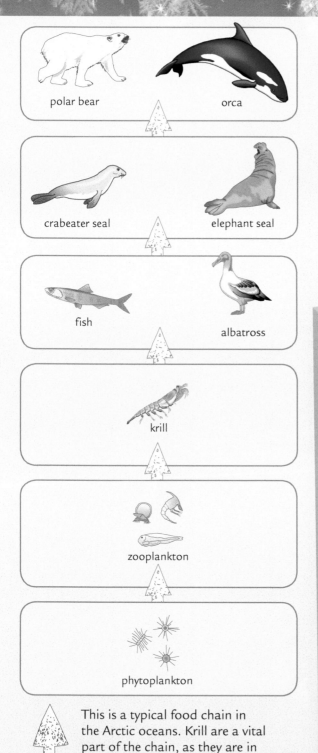

polar bear

orca

crabeater seal

elephant seal

fish

albatross

krill

zooplankton

phytoplankton

This is a typical food chain in the Arctic oceans. Krill are a vital part of the chain, as they are in the Antarctic too — see page 20.

At sea, tiny phytoplankton are eaten by herbivorous (plant-eating) zooplankton. Next in the chain are carnivorous zooplankton, followed by fish and birds, then seals. The top predators are polar bears and orcas (killer whales).

In summer the Arctic has a surprisingly large number of insects buzzing around — Arctic bumble bees, flies, grasshoppers, mosquitoes, and moths.

DID YOU KNOW?

The narwhal is found only in the Arctic. Known as the "unicorn of the sea," this bizarre-looking creature has a long tusk on the front of its head. Narwhals need to come up to the surface to breathe, but sometimes they get stuck under the ice. Several narwhals together can smash through the ice with their foreheads.

ARCTIC ANIMALS — LAND AND SEA

POLAR BEARS

The best way to spot a polar bear in the Arctic landscape is to look for movement. A polar bear is perfectly camouflaged against the snow. It has a big, bulky body with a thick layer of fat and a shaggy coat to repel water and shield it from the icy air. Under its coat, its skin is black to absorb warmth from the Sun.

In addition to seals, polar bears sometimes eat whales, narwhals, and walruses.

Amazing fact

Polar bears are the largest carnivores on Earth. An adult polar bear can measure up to 8 feet, 6 inches (2.6 m) long and weigh around 1,320 pounds (600 kg) – nearly as much as a small car!

The bear glides into the water to hunt seals. Polar bears can swim long distances at 6 miles (10 km) per hour. They paddle with their slightly webbed front paws and hold their hind legs flat like a rudder for steering.

With its acute sense of smell, the polar bear has detected its prey 10 miles (16 km) away. After a long swim, the bear waits by the edge of the ice for the seal to appear. The bear lunges forward to seize it, misses, and the seal escapes. Typical! Polar bears spend more than half of their time hunting but only succeed 2 percent of the time.

DID YOU KNOW?

The seas of the Arctic are home to 17 types of whale, including the beluga whale. The beluga's body is 40–50 percent fat, which helps to keep it warm. This fat store also keeps the whale alive if food is scarce.

Unlike many whales, the beluga can turn its head without having to turn its body, which helps it search all around for its next meal.

ANTARCTIC ANIMALS

In the cold waters of the Antarctic Ocean there are millions of tiny, shrimp-like animals called krill. They play a vital role in the **ecosystem** of the Antarctic. Fish, seals, whales, penguins, and other birds all feast on krill. Blue whales prefer to eat nothing else. They gulp down vast quantities of the creatures with each gigantic mouthful.

These Antarctic krill are feeding on algae growing on the underside of the ice.

Antifreeze life saver

No land-based mammals live on Antarctica, but there are tiny invertebrates (creatures with no backbone) creeping around — mites, ticks, and nematode worms. In winter they freeze in ice under rocks, not moving, eating, or drinking. They have a substance in their bodies that prevents them from freezing — a built-in antifreeze! When the weather warms up, they spring to life again.

DID YOU KNOW?

Pure-white snow petrels breed farther south than any other bird on the planet, mainly on the Antarctic continent. When nesting, mating pairs seek crevices in the rocks that will protect them and their chicks from the biting wind. Snow petrels eat a seafood diet of krill, fish, and squid.

Amazing fact

Adélies mostly feed at the water's surface but can dive down to nearly 600 feet (180 m). That is the depth of 90 Olympic swimming pools!

Adélie penguins

Most people who come to Antarctica want to see the penguins. Adélies are the most common penguins here. Living together in colonies (groups) of up to several thousand, they waddle around and huddle together for warmth. Adélies are excellent swimmers, catching fish and krill for their dinner. A layer of fat keeps the penguin warm in and out of the water.

On a sunny day, these Adélie penguins do not need to huddle together.

WHO LIVES IN THE POLAR LANDS?

LIVING IN THE ARCTIC

It's not easy to travel around the icy landscape of the Arctic. In winter there is little or no daylight, while in summer the Sun shines continuously. Yet more than 4 million people live and thrive in the region.

This map shows where indigenous peoples live in the Arctic.

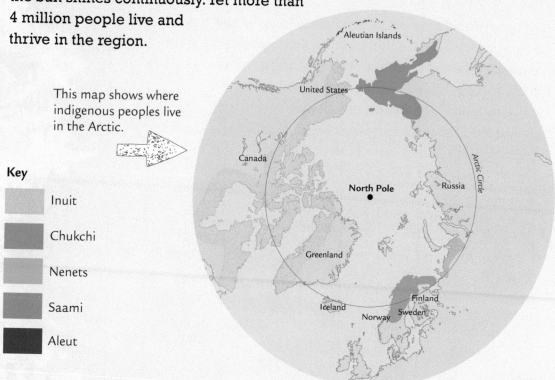

Key

Inuit

Chukchi

Nenets

Saami

Aleut

Aleutian Islands

United States

Canada

North Pole

Russia

Arctic Circle

Greenland

Iceland

Finland

Norway

Sweden

HUNTING, FISHING, AND HERDING

Indigenous peoples have lived in the Arctic for thousands of years. The Saami live in Finland, Sweden, Norway, and Russia. The Nenets and Chukchi are in Russia. The Aleut live in Alaska, and the Inuit in Alaska, Canada, and Greenland. Many were **nomads,** such as the Saami and Nenets, who traveled with their reindeer herds. The Inuit and Aleut hunted and fished to survive. They built small settlements, often close to animals' migration routes and food sources.

DID YOU KNOW?

In the 20th century, many Inuit gave up their traditional way of life and moved to towns to work in mines or oil fields. Some turned to fishing, making handicrafts or working in the tourist industry. The Saami continued their nomadic life until the start of the 21st century, when they too settled in modern houses. Now only Saami herders roam with their reindeer, while their families stay at home.

KEEPING COZY

Long before the days of high-tech fleece, the Inuit made warm clothing to survive the cold. They killed caribou in August, when the animals' hair was short and fine, and used the skins to make garments. In winter, when the hair of caribou and musk oxen was thick, the Inuit hunted them and turned the hides into cozy bedding.

This Inuit woman in Nunavut, Canada, wears a traditional coat made from caribou hide.

THE "LAST NORTH" EXPEDITION TO THE NORTH POLE

In 2014 American polar explorers Eric Larsen and Ryan Waters embarked on an extraordinary expedition. They traveled from the northern tip of Ellesmere Island, Canada, to the geographic North Pole — a 500-mile (800-km) trek. The pair carried all their supplies on two heavy sleds.

TERRIBLE TERRAIN

Larsen and Waters faced the challenges of white-outs (when they could see nothing but snow), ferocious winds, and limited fuel and food. Climate change had made the ice uneven. Ice sheets had smashed together, broken apart, then crashed together again and refrozen, which had created fields of jagged ice.

They traveled on skis but sometimes had to swim through breaks in the ice, tying the sleds together to go through the water. The ice drifted at night, so they sometimes awoke to find they had drifted south and had to cover the distance again. At one terrifying time, they were stalked by a polar bear.

Waters swims across a break in the ice dragging a sled. For longer water crossings, they tied the sleds together to form a raft.

Eric Larsen shows the equipment that was packed into the sleds. The explorers used sleds made from a light material called Kevlar.

SPECIAL GEAR

It was so cold that much regular trekking gear was useless. Rubber on snowshoes gets too brittle at low temperatures, nylon tears, and metal tent poles snap. Larsen and Waters wrapped duct tape around the fuel bottles for their stove to avoid getting frostbite from touching the metal. They replaced the heavy vacuum packaging around their freeze-dried food packets with plastic bags filled with butter and olive oil. These foodstuffs provided useful extra calories as they neared the North Pole.

On May 6, after 53 days on the ice, the explorers finally arrived at the North Pole. Larsen felt that it was one of the most difficult expeditions he had ever done. "You know an expedition is tough when getting stalked by polar bears is the least of your worries," he joked.

WORKING IN THE ANTARCTIC

Although nobody lives in the Antarctic, there are research stations full of scientists studying the weather, biology, geology, oceans, astronomy, and more. They drill and take out **ice cores** to study climate change over long stretches of time and find out how species are affected. To avoid causing further climate change themselves, the stations are built to use energy sources that do not harm the environment. For example, Princess Elisabeth Station was built in 2009 and uses wind and solar power.

A scientist drills a hole in the sea ice to study algae and sea life.

Amazing fact

Antarctica belongs to no country and has no government or police force.

ANTARCTIC LIVING

For a trip to the Antarctic, it's best to wear thick, comfortable coveralls. Devices such as cameras do not work in very low temperatures, so they need to be warmed up with a hand-warmer before they can be used. At night, visitors should exercise before they go to bed to raise their body temperature. They might like to store their clothes under the covers so they can get dressed in bed in the morning.

There is little fresh food because it all has to be flown in, at great cost. Apples and oranges are highly prized treats. All waste has to be flown out in crates. Everyone working in the Antarctic has to look after the environment and should not interfere with the wildlife. Skuas are like seagulls and scavenge food, but people must not scare them away. No one should approach the penguins, no matter how cute they look!

DID YOU KNOW?

Although tourism in Antarctica is tightly controlled, there are more visitors than scientists and they have a heavy impact on the environment. They love to visit wild areas on tour ships, but can disturb the wildlife during the short breeding season and damage fragile habitats by walking around. Ships can have accidents and cause oil spills.

WHAT RESOURCES ARE IN THE POLAR REGIONS?

As the world's known oil and gas supplies are being used up, the **fossil-fuel** industries are scouring remote land and oceans for new sources.

RICHES UNDER THE ICE

Under the icy worlds of the Arctic and Antarctic lie huge supplies of oil, gas, and minerals. Pumping out oil and gas in freezing conditions is difficult and costly, but it's happening nevertheless.

Arctic oil and gas

More than 400 oil and gas fields have been found on the land north of the Arctic Circle, although a quarter are not in production yet. The biggest gas fields are in Alaska and Siberia. Beginning in the late 20th century, oil and gas fields were established on Alaska's North Slope.

This drilling platform is on Alaska's North Slope. The North Slope has some of North America's largest gas deposits.

Mineral treasures

In Russia and northern Canada, mining industries have developed. They unearth the buried treasures of Siberia, central Russia: nickel, gold, silver, and zinc. Gold, coal, and quartz are mined in the polar regions of Canada. Yet many resources remain untouched because they are too hard to access.

Amazing fact

Experts believe that about 13 percent of the world's oil reserves and 30 percent of the world's natural gas are in the Arctic, as yet undiscovered.

HUNTING AND FISHING

Indigenous people have always hunted reindeer, caribou, and polar bears for food and hides. Now, commercial (profit-making) fishing boats sail the Arctic seas catching salmon, cod, and pollock to sell worldwide. Commercial whaling is banned, but whale hunters from Japan, Norway, and Iceland still kill whales for their meat and for use in makeup and health products.

DID YOU KNOW?

About 12,000 years ago, giant woolly mammoths roamed Siberia. Now, as climate change and human activities cause the permafrost to melt, fossilized ivory from ancient mammoth tusks are being found near the surface. Siberian hunters dig them up and sell the ivory for thousands of dollars.

A man from Taimyr, Russia, holds up the giant tusk of a woolly mammoth. Local carvers use the ivory to make jewelry and other items.

ARCTIC OIL FIELDS — PROS AND CONS

For the last 30 years, oil from the Arctic has flowed from a pipeline in Alaska to supply one-fifth of the oil needs of the United States. Alaska depends on oil for one-third of its economic activity.

Now, Arctic warming has reduced the ice cover, so it has become easier to access the region for development. Countries such as China, the United States, and Russia are rushing in to search for energy resources. They believe that the world needs oil for economies to continue to grow, and that drilling for oil will only affect a small part of the Arctic. Oil companies are particularly interested in the waters in the Chukchi and Beaufort seas. In 2015, President Barack Obama agreed that Royal Dutch Shell could start drilling in the Chukchi Sea.

An activist from the environmental campaign group Greenpeace, dressed as a polar bear, is protesting at a German gas station. Greenpeace protests against oil company Shell because it drills in the Arctic.

DESTROYING THE WILDERNESS

Environmental campaigners are worried about the cost to the environment caused by this drilling for oil. They ask: is the world's need for new oil supplies more important than preserving the wilderness? Accidents threaten the region. In 1989 the *Exxon Valdez* spill in Prince William Sound, Alaska, was disastrous for wildlife. The development of oil fields harms native plants, animals, and peoples and deepens climate change.

DID YOU KNOW?

Prudhoe Bay oil field in Alaska causes air **pollution** and **greenhouse gas** emissions. Oil industry constructions sprawl over the Arctic: power plants, roads, pipelines, production works, and living quarters for workers. Tundra wetlands, floodplains, and other **habitats** have been destroyed. Waste and spills from the oil industry have polluted many sites. On average, there is one oil spill per day at Prudhoe Bay. Leaking oil harms fish and wildlife and causes long-term damage to the environment.

EXPLOITING ANTARCTICA

There could be a wealth of fuel and mineral resources in Antarctica, but the subzero temperatures, brief summer, and thick ice make them even harder to extract than in the Arctic.

Coal has been found along the coast of Antarctica. At the moment, however, it's far too expensive to mine and deliver it to other parts of the world. Antarctica might have oil flowing deep below the ice, but no one has explored the possibility — yet.

If we develop enough alternative forms of energy, such as solar and wind power, we can leave such resources under the ground. But if we continue to rely on fossil fuels, energy companies will move into more remote regions — maybe even Antarctica.

Moving icebergs?

People have even considered towing icebergs to provide fresh water to other parts of the world or to use in deep-freeze storage sites for grains and other foods. But the cost of transporting the ice remains too high, and much of it would melt along the way.

Icebergs like this come from glaciers. The glaciers drift toward the sea as frozen rivers over hundreds or thousands of years. Pushed by the ice behind them, the icebergs break off from the glaciers to float in the sea.

Amazing fact

Less than 3 percent of Antarctica is ice-free. The ice of Antarctica contains about 94 percent of all the fresh water on Earth.

Tourism

Increasingly, tourists are visiting this beautiful, wild continent. They can travel by boat along the coast, stopping at research stations and wildlife nesting sites. Some brave individuals embark on expeditions here, in the toughest environment on the planet.

Others take to the skies in private planes. But a tourist flight over Antarctica can be risky. Blizzards and white-outs are frequent and there's no air-traffic control. If a plane was unlucky enough to have an accident, it would be extremely hard to rescue the people on board.

Tourists love to get close to penguins. In Antarctica, penguins tend not to fear humans because there are no predators that hunt them on land.

HOW IS CLIMATE CHANGE AFFECTING THE POLAR REGIONS?

In the Arctic and Antarctic, the effects of climate change can clearly be seen. The sea ice and glaciers are melting, and vast **ice shelves** are breaking away and crashing into the water. Why is it happening so rapidly?

GLOBAL WARMING

Climate change is increased by the albedo effect — how much a surface reflects the Sun's energy. Sea ice reflects about 90 percent of sunlight. Yet open water absorbs about 94 percent of the heat. The ocean becomes warmer, more sea ice melts, more water is exposed, and the process becomes quicker and quicker.

In south Spitsbergen, Norway, the glaciers are retreating. In the past, the bay was frozen over. Now the water is always dotted with icebergs. It used to only be like this in summer.

Amazing fact

Global warming in the Arctic is happening at nearly twice the average rate of the rest of the world.

DID YOU KNOW?

In the Arctic, buildings, roads, and pipelines have been built on the permafrost and they can cause it to thaw. As it thaws, these structures become unstable and can even collapse.

HEATING THE ARCTIC

Carbon dioxide is the gas most usually associated with causing global warming. However, in the Arctic, the permafrost contains **methane,** which holds in more heat than carbon dioxide. Rising temperatures are thawing the permafrost. As it melts it releases methane, which traps more heat. As a result, these regions warm up faster than other regions.

The Arctic oceans are becoming more acidic. That's because there is more carbon dioxide in the atmosphere, and the oceans absorb some of it. The carbon dioxide reacts with the water and makes it acidic. Acidic water affects the development of the shells of animals, including **plankton.** Plankton form the base of the food chain, so any damage to them affects the food supply of all other creatures in the chain.

Arctic plants might be able to adapt to climate change, though. Studies from Norway show that their seeds can travel long distances in the wind, in birds, and on floating sea ice to new areas that have the climate conditions they are adapted for, and where they could take root.

Polar bear SOS

The Arctic ecosystem relies on sea ice, from tiny plankton in the ocean to huge polar bears, the top predators. Yet the sea ice is shrinking dramatically and rapidly.

Polar bears rest on sea ice between bouts of seal hunting, and they breed on the ice. For the last 20 years, the summer sea ice has been shrinking more than before and for a longer period of time during the summer months. This means that there is less ice and the bears have to travel longer distances to find a spot to relax. They are also spending more time on shore, waiting for the sea ice to refreeze so they can hunt again. In the meantime, they rely on their fat stores. Now that there is less ice and it melts for a longer time, they might face starvation — especially in the south, where the sea ice disappears for the longest time. Females with cubs to feed are most at risk.

A polar bear rests on the edge of an ice sheet, north of Svalbard, Norway. Sea ice is reducing and it is also thinner.

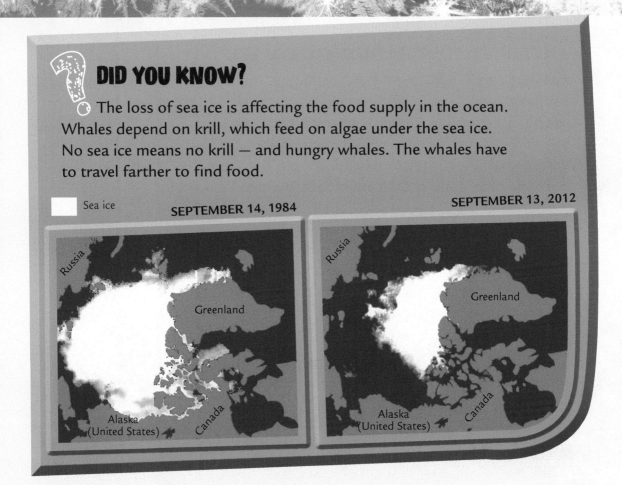

DID YOU KNOW?

The loss of sea ice is affecting the food supply in the ocean. Whales depend on krill, which feed on algae under the sea ice. No sea ice means no krill — and hungry whales. The whales have to travel farther to find food.

Sea ice

SEPTEMBER 14, 1984

SEPTEMBER 13, 2012

Russia
Greenland
Alaska (United States)
Canada

Russia
Greenland
Alaska (United States)
Canada

Being on shore for longer periods of time can lead to clashes with people in coastal communities. Polar bears may attack humans and be shot or illegally hunted by them. Polar bears are now a threatened species.

Drilling and damage

People are adding to the problems of climate change. As more ice melts, new areas of ocean emerge. This makes industrial development at sea easier and allows developers to travel through the new areas of ocean to reach previously unexplored parts of the land. There is likely to be more drilling for oil and gas, which will damage the fragile environment and bring with it the risk of oil spills and disturbing wildlife.

ANTARCTICA'S CHANGING CLIMATE

As in the Arctic, climate change is affecting Antarctica. It's a vast continent, and the effects vary from place to place. In some areas the sea ice is increasing. Yet the west coast of the Antarctic Peninsula is one of the fastest-warming areas on the planet. It's heating up at five times the average rate of global warming! The Antarctic Ocean is also warming more rapidly than other oceans around the world.

Ice shelf collapse

In this remote region, enormous ice shelves (the floating extensions of ice sheets on the ground) can sometimes be seen breaking away and crashing into the ocean. In some places the ice shelves have slowly shrunk over decades. In others, they have collapsed quickly and dramatically.

Could the retreat of the ice shelves be part of the natural changes in climate? Most scientists don't think so. Researchers found that some of the disappearing ice shelves had been there for at least 10,000 years — until human-made global warming destroyed them.

This photo shows a vast area of sea ice in Antarctica that shattered into smaller pieces within 24 hours in 2010. Warmer summer temperatures are causing more and more ice shelves to collapse.

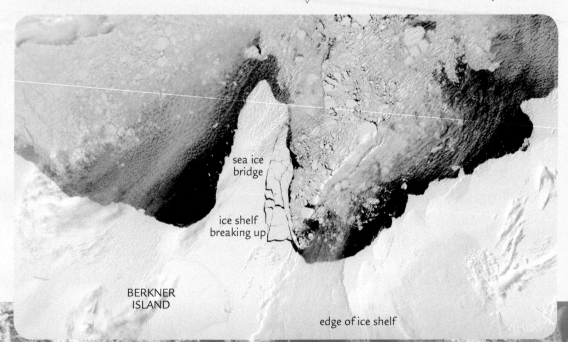

sea ice bridge

ice shelf breaking up

BERKNER ISLAND

edge of ice shelf

Amazing fact

If the Antarctic ice sheet melted completely, sea level worldwide could rise by more than 200 feet (60 m).

Wildlife under threat

Over a long period, the krill population has been falling as the sea ice retreats, threatening the food supply of whales, seals, and penguins. The number of Adélie penguins is decreasing. Emperor penguins could decline by 95 percent by the end of the 21st century if the sea ice continues to shrink at the current rate. The melting of snow and ice has allowed more plants to grow in Antarctica. As in the Arctic, it looks like plants might benefit from climate change.

Sights like these could become a thing of the past. Since 2011, there has been a major decline in the penguin population of Antarctica. For example, a huge iceberg in Cape Denison, eastern Antarctica, cut off the penguins' route to the sea. The population of 160,000 has been reduced to 10,000.

CLIMATE CHANGE AND ANTARCTIC PENGUINS

Researchers at Biscoe Point, near Palmer Station, first spotted Gentoo penguins in 1993. Since then, as the sea ice has retreated, Gentoo penguins have settled at Palmer Station, while Adélie penguins have been disappearing. What is going on?

Palmer Station, near the tip of the Antarctic Peninsula, is about 700 miles (1,100 km) south of Tierra del Fuego. In January 2015 Cornell Lab science editor Hugh Powell traveled there with a group of researchers, riding on inflatable boats. On the shoreline, Gentoos were everywhere. The team guessed there were about 3,600 nests.

TAGGING PENGUINS

On a hectic schedule, the researchers visited 21 islands every three days to study the penguins and other wildlife. They caught some penguins and attached satellite tags, depth recorders, and radio transmitters, marking each bird with a green wax cattle marker so it would be easy to spot and remove the devices three days later. From the data, researchers learned where the penguins fed, how deep they dived, and how long they stayed away.

Antarctic researchers attach a tracker and depth recorder to a penguin. The tracker stores data that can later be downloaded to a computer. The depth recorder sends a signal every second that the penguin is in the water.

Amazing fact

There are 17 species of penguin in the world. Seven of them nest on the Antarctic continent and islands.

CLIMATE CHANGE, NOT COMPETITION

The scientists learned that it is climate change driving the Adélies away rather than competition from Gentoos. Adélies live in a sea-ice habitat. They need to be on ice and lay eggs on the snow. But Gentoos wait for the snow to melt to lay their eggs. Palmer Station is now free of sea ice for 100 days more each year than it was 35 years ago. It's no longer a suitable breeding place for Adélies, but it is perfect for Gentoos.

A female Adélie penguin sits on her eggs. Adélies usually lay two eggs, and the chicks are born after just over a month.

HOW CAN WE PROTECT THE ARCTIC AND ANTARCTIC?

The polar regions are under threat from pollution, overfishing, and invasive species. By far the biggest threat is climate change. What can we do? The problems could be tackled step by step.

We could introduce protected ocean areas to defend large parts of Antarctica from overfishing and pollution. Countries need to work together to do this. They could all agree to catch fewer fish. Because chemicals in the air and the water can spread from one area to another and affect the polar regions, countries should try to reduce pollution in general. These simple measures would allow fish stocks and the ecosystem to recover, and the protected areas could become refuges for species at risk.

In the Cooper Bay and Cooper Island protected area, in South Georgia, Antarctica, people are forbidden to harm animals or damage the environment, and the number of visitors is strictly limited.

DID YOU KNOW?

The Ross Sea is a bay in southern Antarctica. In contrast to much of Antarctica, sea ice on the surface of the Ross Sea is growing and lasting for a longer season. Scientists think this is because of changes in the strength of the winds that blow around the region. Preserving this region could create another safe haven for wildlife endangered by climate change elsewhere.

Protecting Antarctica from invasive species shouldn't be too hard. Sometimes, visitors bring in seeds by accident on their clothes and equipment. There are now rules to prevent this. For example, people are not allowed to bring soil to Antarctica in case it contains plant seeds or insect eggs. People need to be more careful when coming to this sensitive region.

OUR FUTURE

In the long term, we have no choice but to reduce greenhouse-gas emissions. In the Antarctic, people should use only wind and solar energy and transportation methods that cause as little damage as possible. But to really make a difference, we need to reduce greenhouse gas emissions worldwide.

FOR BETTER, FOR WORSE

The polar regions are warming, putting wildlife and people's livelihoods at risk. The **exploitation** of resources is multiplying the problem. What are the worst and best possible outcomes?

Worst case

In the worst case, the drive to extract fossil fuels at any cost continues. Major drilling for oil and gas and mining for mineral resources take place in the Arctic and Antarctic. Pipelines, roads, and buildings are constructed, destroying the natural environment. Wildlife habitats are lost, and indigenous Arctic peoples are forced out.

Tourism also expands. Antarctica becomes a major center for skiing and mountaineering, with new airstrips and hotels damaging the environment and creating waste.

The fragile environment is damaged; invasive species multiply; plants are destroyed; and penguins' nesting sites are disturbed.

People love to ski in remote areas. Travel companies already advertise skiing trips to Antarctica for experienced ski mountaineers seeking a challenge.

Best outcome

The best outcome would be if countries of the world decide to leave polar oil and gas underground, to avoid further climate change. Instead, they turn to alternative fuel sources for all their energy needs. Only environmentally friendly research is allowed, and the wildlife of the polar regions gradually recovers.

Fur seals bask close to a large iceberg on Adelaide Island, Antarctica. The future of the wildlife of the polar regions is uncertain.

45

GLOSSARY

algae simple plants with no leaves, stems, or roots, which grow in or near water

altitude height above sea level

blubber fat of sea animals

current movement of water in the seas, oceans, and large lakes

ecosystem plants and animals living in a particular area and the environment in which they live

Equator imaginary line around the middle of Earth

exploitation act of using something in an unfair or unjust way for selfish reasons

fossil fuel fuel such as coal or oil that was formed over millions of years from the remains of animals or plants

greenhouse gas gas such as carbon dioxide or methane that warms Earth by releasing heat into the atmosphere (the gases around Earth)

hibernate to spend the winter in a state like deep sleep

ice cap covering of ice at the North and South Poles

ice core cylinder-shaped sample of ice drilled from an ice sheet for studying

ice shelf thick layer of ice on land that extends over a large area of sea

ice sheet thick layer of ice that covers land, often found in polar regions

indigenous one of the original peoples of a land

latitude distance of a place north or south of the Equator

lichen simple, slow-growing gray or yellow plant that spreads over the surface of rocks, walls, and trees and does not have any flowers

methane greenhouse gas that greatly adds to global warming when it is released into the atmosphere

moss small green or yellow plant without flowers; in the polar regions it lives on rocks and on the ground

nomad someone who moves from place to place in search of grazing land

perennial (of plants) living for several years

plankton very small forms of plant and animal life that live in the sea or fresh water and on which many animals feed

pollution harmful or poisonous substances in the air or water or on land

prevailing wind wind that blows from a particular direction

tundra large, flat Arctic regions of northern Europe, Asia, and North America where no trees grow and there is permafrost; the surface layer above the permafrost melts in the summer

READ MORE

BOOKS

Arctic and Antarctic. Eyewitness. New York: DK Children, 2012.

Hardyman, Robyn. *Surviving the Ice.* Sole Survivor. New York: Gareth Stevens Publishing, 2016.

Shuckburgh, Emily, and Catherine Chambers. *Polar Scientist. The Coolest Jobs on the Planet.* Chicago: Raintree, 2015.

Spilsbury, Louise. *Polar Regions.* Research on the Edge. Mankato, Minn.: Smart Apple Media, 2016.

Waldron, Melanie. *Polar Regions.* Habitat Survival. Chicago: Raintree, 2013.

FACTHOUND

Use Facthound to find Internet sites related to this book.

Just type in 9781484637845 and go!

PLACE TO VISIT

Live from the Poles: Partner Museums

www.polardiscovery.whoi.edu/museums/index.html

Arctic and Antarctic research expeditions in partnership with science museums across the USA.

INDEX